praise for FIST

Emily Wall's *Fist* is quite remarkable. Remarkable in that it paints a poetic picture of Georgia O'Keeffe not only as artist but also as the seminal person, the feminist and visionary, she was. It's remarkable, too, in its lyric form—how the language and lines diverge and meet, dip across the page (one imagines like O'Keeffe's paintbrush, perhaps), and in the end become their own vocabulary of art and artist. Not just the artistry of Georgia O'Keefe, but the artistry of Emily Wall, an accomplished poet, teacher, mother, feminist, visionary. *Fist* is a rich and necessary collection that proves there is no hard line between canvas and memory, language and light, landscape and love.

— Simmons Buntin, Editor-in-Chief, Terrain.org

Dear Canyon, Dear Fist, Dear Dark Slit, Dear Walking Out, Dear Holy…. the poems of *Fist* give voice and, yes, song, to Georgia O'Keeffe's paintings. In these chronological ekphrastic poems (each one anchored by a specific painting), Wall has found a way to sing Georgia O'Keeffe's life anew through her canvases. The book moves episodically, pointlistically, from moment to moment in O'Keeffe's life and work. Wall's poems are both question and answer. "—dear claw—/—how sharply beautiful I am—," Wall writes. And these honed poems both acknowledge and turn away from the painful misogyny in O'Keeffe's life. They take her experiences and hone them to blades. Painting by painting, Wall's poems honor O'Keeffe's vision and, too, free themselves from it and explore the wilder mysteries of her work.

— Elizabeth Bradfield, author of *Toward Antarctica* and *Theorem*

fist

emily wall

MINERVA RISING PRESS

Boca Raton

Cover art by Georgia O'Keeffe
Book design by Brooke Schultz

ISBN 978-1-950811-15-1

Printed and bound in USA
First Printing March 2022

Published by Minerva Rising Press
17717 Circle Pond Ct
Boca Raton, FL 33496

Sister
this is written for you
who is both song
and fist.

This is also for Corey,
and my three fierce girls,
Acey, Ellie, and Lucy.

Fist is part of a chapbook trilogy written in the wake of the 2016 election. Encapsulating the voices of three powerful women: Mary, mother of Jesus; Georgia O'Keeffe, artist and feminist pioneer; and Alice Waters, chef and food activist. Through persona poems, each book seeks to speak to and lift up women, who are living with trauma and fear, in this current political climate.

Flame, another book in the trilogy, is also available from Minerva Rising press.

contents

About these poems

These poems are ekphrastic, epistolic, persona poems.

Ekphrastic: each poem responds to one piece of Georgia O'Keeffe's art. In my study I have a wall of her paintings — each one printed out, rising up toward the ceiling. I've lived with and worked under these images for the past few years, letting her colors and shapes and vision guide me. I began each piece with one of her paintings, each poem coming forward in the house of that original work. Paired with each poem is the title of a painting I encourage you to look up. It will make your experience richer to have both pieces in front of you.

Epistolic: Georgia was a prolific letter writer in her life; she is perhaps best known for her letters to her husband. They did not live together for much of Georgia's life. These poems are letters, but instead of being to a person, they are to the objects and natural world elements that she painted or found important. Sometimes the poems are to parts of her own body. I was fortunate enough to spend an afternoon in her Abiquiu house. It's filled with the objects that I believe guided her work: rocks, bones, jars of food in the pantry. If you go yourself, you'll see them all still there.

Persona: I've borrowed the "mask" of Georgia to tell her story, and of course my own story. This is the magic of persona poems to me: they allow us to enter our own stories in a safe way, and they encourage us to blend our stories and songs. In studying Georgia's life, I've found the story of a fierce woman, who understood how important it is to find your true home, to live your own life, and to choose what matters to you, even if those around you can't see it, oppose your decisions, or simply dismiss you and your work. Georgia has given me courage, and I hope that she will give you courage too.

PART 1

Amarillo, Texas

One morning as I climbed to the top floor for the Life Class,
there [Eugene Speicher] sat with his fresh linen smock,
blocking the whole stairway and threatening
that he would not let me pass unless I promised to pose for him.
I was annoyed and wanted to go up to work.

'It doesn't matter what you do,' he said.
'I'm going to be a great painter
and you will probably end up
teaching in some girls' school.'

— *Georgia O'Keeffe*, Georgia O'Keeffe

DEAR WIND—

Abstraction with Curve and Circle

dear bone breeze—

you take every part
—of the wide sky—
funnel it down my neck.

Covered in dust, walking down Amarillo

—this sky tracks these canyons—
of throat, rib cage, anklebone.

To taste these layers
of hide and feather—yes.

You gather the calls
of the mama cattle—

looking for their children in the long Texas night.

Passing trains dampen their voices
—those long wheels of men—

—but listen.   Iron bodies always pass.

And then—you
bring back that song
of longing we know so well.

Come wind—
       give names to the bones
             —of my face.

Give shape to the hide
             —of my desire.

             Give rise to these feathers
             —now unbound.

DEAR GREEN—

Blue Lines X

—dear tall swamp, dear salesmen of place
    —I hate you.

Dear empty pantry, dear sick mother—

    —I hate the bending grass lines
                of you

      —of this peeling skin house
             this buried in trees house
      —of these lung-thick clouds.
        I hate this meal of buttered peas!

                (Georgia, it's just a house.)

    And now rain in leaves of corn, spray of dirt on floor

—look:
      how is it the plume I love?

          Spiral from a cow's hooves
            flume of evening light on sky—

if only rain were dust.   Hush.

I snap your necks, stems of green.
I crush you in my teeth, sweet peas—
—Virginia, that put her knee in the small
of my back.

My thighbone is blue, I'm sure of it—
—this indigo core, un-pourable.

The puddle of blood—
from my mother's lungs—

landlady, hand outstretched for her money, framed in a doorway of richest
Virginia green.

I pack up these hands
made of dust.

I'm almost gone.

I will not let you tell me, where to live
what thickness to love.

DEAR QUIET—
Blue Lines X

—dear curled blue—
　　　　　how I've missed you.

　　　I claim you again
　　　　　　—here in this tender puddle

　　　　—there—
　　　in this spoon of moon
　　　　　　　　soft light, long night rising—.

　Beyond
a whole street of chatter, back and forth—like the clicking
　　of branches—a rainstorm
　　　　　　　slam shatter—shades raised—

　　　those lit windows!

　　　　　　　　Just twist away—
　　　　　　　　　—find refuge in a stone
　　　　　　　　　　that fits your fist.

　　　After a long day of
students, questions, gossip
　　　and the bank teller who believes you owe him
　　　　　　　　　—talk—.

　　　Don't be deceived, sister.

You don't owe
    —that man—
        any part of you.

You can live
    curved
in your own
    bone pocket
  —all day—
        if you want.

If he reaches in
    —spin away.

PART 2:
New York City, New York

All the male artists I knew, of course,
made it very plain that as a woman
I couldn't make it—
I might as well stop painting.

—*Georgia O'Keeffe,* Portrait of an Artist

Dear Shutter Eye—
Nude Series

dear muscle slant, dear arch, hand on frame
my back arced—
dear delicious knee!

He sees me: (my love)

I eat stories of vermillion
of Paris, of shadows of rues of cigarettes of deep wine—

(lie back)—

(hold still   my love   (my rising) you, on white).

(How does it feel—here)?

(And here?)

He hands me a chopstick
—one snow pea—
he hands me a branch
—of cherry blossoms—

just (lie back).

He hangs me—   here   and here—.

                                    (Yes. You on white.)

                    I try a bite—

and look: I have   a small, bright room, the largest wall to paint
                                    any color I desire—.

(Hold still now   my love   my life.)

          Me on white.

          Still.

DEAR FIST—

Black Iris III

dark iris—

—dear hush of a florist door—

here, a moment
of black—
—of velvety quiet.

Down the road
Stieglitz is shot through with some bright light
splayed across marble table, Chinese food
—men crushing words
(her paintings)
(symbolizing)
(the unpronounceable archetypal—)
(—well actually)

I slip past—

—down the long bone of road—

—here—the lift.

The tip of a feather—

the slip of a breeze—

almost missed—

           the angle of a brush
                 that says
                   —it's like this—

                 that says

          your core
        is not a vagina.

      It's a hard bulb
      —a black rock—
      packed like a ribcage

        —before breath.

DEAR CANYON—

Untitled, City Night

                      of stars—
I see you.

                  —I see the light of your bones
                           the halos of your throats—

                  you four, strung high—

above the dark towers

                  those shafts
        of planted steel

                  —every few feet in this city—
                a bragging of pounding.

                —I want to hang this star between two windows—

                      (absolutely not)

                  —his hands bracing the doorway—

                (and why do you always wear black?)

So I hang instead—
        the rising
            —between my legs.

Sister, let them have the stars.

Our rising is so big
          it can't be named.

              Our rising is so bright

                  it pulls the sea—

                      over every dark shore.

DEAR CLOSED—
Slightly Open Shell

dear shell
—dear shimmer, eye under lid

— dear still core—
of breath under rib

sometimes
you must close.

His letters follow me all night
up the corridor of New York
up to the edge of sea—

—thank god for telegrams
a shoreline of rocks, all those lovely
stops.

I'm not. Coming back. Yet.

Listen, little clam, little sliver,
you fingernail
of shimmer—

you can refuse

to open.

You are building
the floor of the entire sea.

You can refuse to spread
your white wings.

Listen: you can keep
that pearl of light

— all to yourself.

PART 3

Lake George, New York

If I stop to think of what others—
authorities—would say...
I'd not be able to do anything.

— *Georgia O'Keeffe,* Georgia O'Keeffe: A Life

DEAR CLEAVE—

Abstraction IX

dear blade and skin—

> I split your apple thighs
> creamy, juicy.

I eat your wide sky
> white lines.

In Lake George a stove—
> for the first time a kitchen
and mine.

> I put pan on flame—sugar in pan—

—apple slices soften in heat.

Dark core
road North.   (We're home.)

> But—I fill my pockets with seeds
> —abandon dark lake for bright

ocean—
> for waves of sharp taste

and under my heels
the crunch and bite
> of salty rock.

(Come home.)

Tender brush, hard frame—
stroke and *snap*.

Return to burner
—to flame—
to hypnotizing white

arched back
tongue curl

(you're my—)

—apple girl, summer girl, split right down the middle girl—

spicy, sweet.

Now retreat.

DEAR PERFECTION—

Peach and Glass

—dear hand on knee bone
                    —peach on dish.

                Dear ancestral kitchen,
                            fragile china,
                                    white-frame farmhouse.
                                        He calls me his (white one).

                    We have such a long history of erasing
                            peaches with our mouths.

                    I spend all day mixing the color
                        of this thin skin—

I'll know it when I see it.

                            (Hold your hands)
                            (exactly) (this way)

                            —he says, over and over—

                            —to me—
                —to the naked girl standing in the frigid lake—
                            his newest model
                            his youngest girl yet.

        Let's just say it:

blue skin
black lake
dark woods—

once upon a time—
there was a girl.

Once upon a time—
—I spent four days perfecting the blush of a peach—

ah. I see it now.

Perfection?

Dark pit
on a white plate.

DEAR DARK SLIT—

Storm Cloud, Lake George

— between deep lake and thick sky—

—Stieglitz photographs
another girl—
bend of knee against thigh

—grass, lake—
such a perfect fold—
(now hold)

—a slice of rain
flashes green

—there—

—is always a fresher sky being born.

Always
a more beautiful hipbone—
rising into notice
at the dinner table, rising for another
glass of dark

—everyone's heads turn—

was that a shard of thunder?

The black seams of me—
                neck-hollow, knee-bend—
                the long lake between my legs—
named and framed.

           How did I come to hang here?

       I fold my napkin.

Look: somewhere

        —a wave of wind begins.

           A curve so wild

              I could climb inside it.

Dear Unfulring—
Special No. 40

dear soupy air—slumping hospital walls—

here I swallow salt—
—swallow sky—
sea-green—milky blue
here my heels sink
in a million fragments of softened bone—

(this is what you want).

If I still had a core
I might be made of coral.

(Bermuda will cure you, you'll see)
Trust me.

Even one shard
—one jagged point—
would work.

But everything between me is all air, all—

(diagnosis: psychoneurosis)
all tropical flower.

Just—lift—your brush—

Him hushing
the offer for me to paint Radio City Music Hall—

(trust me, this is what she wants)

(petals!)

(honey: unfold).

Instead I polish
—the keys of my teeth—
one by one.

In my sleep

—I eat—
a thousand tiny bodies.

In my sleep,

I build a home
out of pure heat.

DEAR BROKEN—

Cow's Skull with Calico Roses

Go.

Hang a cow skull
—dead center—

—scare everyone away—

white flame
of bone.

—They say it's about balance—

one sharp horn
on each side

of your life.

On the left, the blossom of marriage

—and a housekeeper, who is horrified when she returns
to a skull on the table.

But on the right—oh—

        —a white road

            —a sharpening point.

A pinprick of light.

PART 4:
Taos, New Mexico

Before I put a brush to canvas,
I question, 'Is this mine?...
Is it influenced by some idea which I have acquired from some man?'...
I am trying with all my skill
to do a painting that is all of women,
as well as all of me.

— *Georgia O'Keeffe*, Portrait of an Artist

DEAR PETAL SOFT—

Banana Flower II

—dear gorgeous
  rot—   I am done with you.

Dear velvet core——
   dear pillow talk
     thighs unfurling—

      I am done with you.

Dear snowy lake, quilted March

    dear rich soil,
      you green leaves of corn—

      I am done with you too.

    Dear halo of streetlights—
—dear muffins dear sugar, small talk, needy men gallery lights, greedy name—

    you too.

I want hard dirt
                    dry sky.

One red
            hot pepper

                                    I've grown myself.

Dear dirt-crusted
knucklebone—
                you, I adore.

DEAR STAR PRICK—

Black Cross with Stars and Blue

dear night
last light,
dear blue illumination—

I peel off every shiver.
Arms now wide in warm dirt.

Here, blue-green sage
tide-rises sand—
and curves of wind.

A black shadow
washes across my ribcage—

a hawk, a cross

a monk singing
somewhere
behind me.

One star prick in each palm
—a thousand miles between the poles of my life—

(come home).

A crush of dust
in fist

and my first prayer is—

let me bury all these nail holes,

all these stars.

All these tiny, bright graves.

DEAR FERAL SELF—

Eagle Claw and Bean Necklace

—dear claw—
—how sharply beautiful I am—

and
—how beautifully sharp— you see? I can speak again.

New York is so far away.

Here—I am windowsills
rich with my walks: shells, bones, stones—

here—   I am
light falling on
palm pads, leaping tendons

—this warm belly—
shelled egg

I'm no longer afraid
will break.

Of course they will try.

So line your bedside table with seeds—

and remember—   how last night
                    —you sat up in the desert
                    moonlight

                    —your body the only drop of water

for miles—your eye, shining—.

            Now, sharpen—
                        to a gleaming point—
                                    your tongue bone.

            Sister—first curl, then strike.

PART 5

Ghost Ranch, New Mexico

Living out there
has just meant happiness.
Sometimes I think I'm half mad
with love for this place.

—*Georgia O'Keeffe*, Portrait of an Artist

DEAR THIN AIR—

Ladder to the Moon

evening sky

—largest quiet, deepest canvas—

dear rungs to that blue door.

Tonight I wait for a friend,
the stones of the patio cooling.

I feel better when I put my hands
on these solid sides

on the ribs of this rising—.

If you look hard enough at the moon,
it will outshine—
the stars

those holes through which his
letters drop, suddenly.

(Please! My little one,
my white one,
I need you
come back down
please.)

Of course
—it's the grip—

hand on rung-bone—
        it's the looking up.

                Tonight I wait for a friend
             the stones of the patio cooling—

    —my feet arcing into darkness.

                Oh, forget whoever it is
                  you are waiting for.

Tonight, here is a ladder—
      half bright with your climbing—

and half dark
      with your promise.

DEAR GRAIN OF LIGHT—

Pelvis Series, Red with Yellow

dear corn, dear cob
dear bending green blades—

how full of silk you are—
how flush with sugar—
now this delicious stripping!

For years I painted
your unpeeling.

Now I wonder:

why not your kernels?

These golden stones—
these bright vertebrae!

But instead— I roast you in the adobe
stove, stir you into soup
sharp with chilies.

I soften you with heat—
then crush you with my eager teeth.

Ah, I see it now.

Tender bodies—
    softened spine—

              I could never hang you
                on my wall.

DEAR HOT COAL—

Stump in Red Hills

I touch you.

                Everyone looks past you—
                    into the rising of hill and sky—

what
are they looking for?

                There—one tree!
                    One green canyon
                      a mist of water
                          one fragile desert bloom.

But it's the hard bulb
      I want—

        —the deep curve, the cored home—
                    —it's the marrow I crave.

        I crumble a handful into my paint
                —touch it to tongue—

                —here, I taste the lasting.

This morning I stand in my biggest window

                         —sun hot on my canvas—

      and watch the road, the crowd
           as they drive by, their plume
                    eaten by the long sky—.

    Gone.

Now—

    I step out into this canvas of dust.

                    I shrug off every shadow
                      until I'm just skin

       just heat—
           until I'm only—

               tongue and brush.

               Bone and flame.

DEAR WALKING OUT—
Winter Road

                        Of course we live
                in houses made of dust.

                  I lean naked
           early evening, backbone

    to softening
      adobe—
                yesterday, a little rain
                        today, a weakening.

    I touch my skin—   its hundred tiny scars—

        its thousand broken roads.

    I trace this falling—   this dissolving—

        a muscle beginning—to let go.

Tomorrow, I will walk out
                      —in first light—

and I will find bright
bones.

I will gather them—
these not-deaths,
these moon-shards, survivors,
these teeth-in-wind.

Tomorrow I will paint them—

and paint them again—

until every petal of skin

is peeled away.

PART 6:

Abiquiu, New Mexico

It is a way for me to live very comfortably·
at the tail end of the earth
so far away that hardly any one will ever come to see me
and I like it.

—*Georgia O'Keeffe*, Georgia O'Keeffe and Her Houses

DEAR ROOFLESS ROOM—

The White Place—A Memory

dear rib cage of sky—

—here, I can kneel.

White walls
        thick *vigas*, windows
that sweep wide
        to pure rock, luscious light—

finally.

Why did it take me so long?
        Dark sky, deep lake
    all those frigid baptisms.

I scrape down every wall
        until my whole view is

mud
straw
sky.

Here, my psalm—

bare skin
biting teeth
walking feet.

I place one blade
      of bone
    in this square
     of light.

                I welcome the snakes
                   who want to live
                      in my fireplace.

          Sister: in this paradise
     we walk out, and we find our own

             rib bones—
               —our own names—

     for these stunning

        dust-built
        bodies.

DEAR SACRAMENT—

White Patio with Red Door

—dear pantry shelves

—dear January day of glass jars—

the colors!
　　　　Vermillion, melon, indigo

—just waiting
　　　　for my need.

Each *viga* painted, floor clean—
　　　　see what hangs
　　　　on my true skeleton?

Sister, what hangs on yours?

Who do you invite
past your front door?

Past the table and chairs
　　　　—the kitchen stove—

past the ingredients in your pot
that say so much
about you.

What do you keep
    in the room
built only to hold
        —your hunger?

In mine?
            A ribcage of shelves

                    a thousand glass sheaths.

                        One lantern
                        of squash
                    of warmest orange.

DEAR ROSARY—
Black Rock with Blue III

—black rock—dark in pocket—

> dear thumb bone
> soothed against your edge.

They say I'm a parlor game
—a mystery—

> (let's put this rock on a table
> see if Georgia steals it).

They think it's funny
I must have it.

> (Georgia, it's just a rock.)

Listen: if you find your rock

> on someone's glass table—

> —take it.

The mystery is this:

       a prayer is not
              words in wind, a chant by men—

but your reach—

            hard and dark.

Both song
       and fist.

DEAR JUST OUTSIDE—

Black Door with Snow

dear black door, holy door
  —dear opening—

        —dear dark of thought.

            I've painted this craving
                a thousand times.

    Do you know this? I think you do.

            We see a door in the vast sky of this world—
                    and we must
                walk through it
                        under it—
                a bone arch, a flowering vine
                        a silver gate.

We name it again
            and again—

    with our brushes, with our songs—

                and we never get it right.

        So—
    we pause.

Maybe better not
                to unlatch
        the heavy handle
    —iron against cold wood—

                as snow begins to blossom—

better not to step
            into that deep wild.

                    We simply stand
                            —just outside—

            —snow petals melting—
        in our thirsty hands.

DEAR HOLLY—

Abstraction

—monastery song—

                             dark bell
                                  deep arch

—it all arcs inward—

                —I touch fingertip to swirl
                   of ear—
                         to shuttered eye
                              now blind.

My foot follows —
        this river of rock
marking the edge
        of my garden path.

                   I empty my palm
           of the last stone.   Begin my last *kinhin*.

Breathe in
breath out.

               Is two the holy number? The way
                a heart beats, the yin yang?

            Of course we show the soul
                —as a crossroads—
             white cross on blue sky.

Say instead: it's a wind twist—a curve—
              peach pit, clam shell,
                    pelvis.

                              Cup of fist
                              and palm.

    In clay—I trace the promise
of a long road, winding into infinite hills.

            It's not the living I'll miss—

                        but the way my fingers—

                              ring the deep song
                              of everything.

PART 7:
The Far Away

When I think of death, I only regret
that I will not be able to see
this beautiful country anymore

—*Georgia O'Keeffe*, Portrait of an Artist

DEAR FAR AWAY—

Pelvis with Blue

—dear blue song—
        dust caress—

        I travel through the canyons
           of each fingertip
   —sweet with sage.

        The back of my hand
           a map of the red hills I climbed—

   the time I slept
        under the pinyon, wild in the wind—
           —scent of deep—snow
              in the indigo air.

    I remember.

The rush of wind in lungs
        when I cross the world of sky and heat

   and there, the one wing—
        —of bone—   I didn't even know
             I was looking for

now found—
    and carried—
        all the way home.

        Now, I trace its deep
            curve—

      this pelvis, this cradle
      — this very center—

      that tethers me
          to forever.

End Notes & Sources

These poems are ekphrastic, responding to specific works of Georgia's art.

Dear Wind: *Abstraction with Curve and Circle*, 1916
Dear Green: *Blue Lines X*, 1916
Dear Quiet: *Blue II*, 1916

Dear Shutter Eye: *Nude Series*, 1917
Dear Fist: *Black Iris III*, 1926
Dear Canyon: *Untitled, City Night*, 1970
Dear Closed: *Slightly Open Shell*, 1926

Dear Cleave: *Abstraction IX*, 1916
Dear Perfection: *Peach and Glass*, 1927
Dear Dark Slit: *Storm Cloud, Lake George*, 1923
Dear Unfurling: *Special No. 40*, 1934
Dear Broken: *Cow's Skull with Calico Roses*, 1931

Dear Petal Soft: *Banana Flower II*, 1934
Dear Star Prick: *Black Cross with Stars and Blue*, 1929
Dear Feral Self: *Eagle Claw and Bean Necklace*, 1934

Dear Thin Air: *Ladder to the Moon*, 1958
Dear Corn: Pelvis Series, *Red with Yellow*, 1945
Dear Hot Coal: *Stump in Red Hills*, 1940
Dear Walking Out: *Winter Road*, 1963

Dear Roofless Room: *The White Place—A Memory*, 1934
Dear Sacrament: *White Patio with Red Door*, 1960
Dear Rosary: *Black Rock with Blue III*, 1970
Dear Just Outside: *Black Door with Snow*, 1955
Dear Holy: *Abstraction*, 1980

Dear Far Away: *Pelvis with Blue*, 1944

Research for this manuscript came from the following texts:

Portrait of an Artist, Laurie Lisle

Georgia O'Keeffe, Roxana Robinson

Georgia O'Keeffe and Her Houses, Barbara Buhler Lynes and Agapita Judy Lopez

Georgia O'Keeffe Museum Collections, Barbara Buhler Lynes

Georgia O'Keeffe Living Modern, Wanda M. Corn

Georgia O'Keeffe and New Mexico: A Sense of Place, Barbara Buhler Lynes Lesley Poing-Kempes, and Frederick W. Turner

My Faraway One: Selected Letters of Georgia O'Keeffe and Alfred Stieglitz, Ed. by Sarah Greenough

A Painter's Kitchen: Recipes from the Kitchen of Georgia O'Keeffe, Margaret Wood

Georgia O'Keeffe: Art and Letters, Jack Cowart and Juan Hamilton with Sarah Greenough

Dinner with Georgia O'Keeffe, Robyn Leah

Georgia O'Keefe: A Portrait by Alfred Stieglitz, forward by Maria Morris Hambourg

Georgia O'Keeffe: The poetry of things, Elizabeth Hutton Turner

Adobe research: https://folklife-media.si.edu/docs/festival/program-book-articles/FESTBK1981_08.pdf

Acknowledgements

My thanks to the following publications in which these poems first appeared, sometimes in different form:

- "Dear Fist" in *Terrain.org*
- "Dear Perfection" in *Terrain.org*
- "Dear Thin Air" in *Terrain.org*
- "Dear Walking out" in *Terrain.org*
- "Dear Sacrament" in *Terrain.org*
- "Dear Roofless Room" in *EcoTheo Review*
- "Dear Cleave" in *Minerva Rising*
- "Dear Green" in *Alaska Women Speak*
- "Dear Shutter Eye" in *Alaska Women Speak*
- "Dear Canyon" in *Alaska Women Speak*

Thank you to the Rasmuson Foundation and the Individual Artist Award program for generously supporting the writing of this book.

A deep thanks to Kim Brown at Minerva Rising Press and her fierce determination to lift up the stories of women. My gratitude to the brilliant work of the Minerva team: Sonya Lara, Kami Westoff, Abby Lewis, and Brooke Schultz who each made this book better.

And finally, thank you to poets Jude Nutter (and the Loft Literary Center), Sandra Beasley, and Dr. James Englehardt who read early versions of these poems.

About the Author

Emily Wall holds an M.F.A. in poetry and is a Professor of English at the University of Alaska. Her poems have been published in journals across the US and Canada and have been nominated for multiple Pushcart Prizes. She is the recipient of several artist grants, including a Rasmuson Individual Artist Award. Her most recent book, *Flame*, won the Minerva Rising chapbook prize. She has two full-length poetry collections published with Salmon Poetry: *Liveaboard and Freshly Rooted*. Emily lives and writes in Douglas, Alaska and she can be found online at www.emily-wall.com.

www.ingramcontent.com/pod-product-compliance
Lightning Source LLC
Chambersburg PA
CBHW032005060426
42449CB00031B/504